notes from an oxygen seeker

notes from an oxygen seeker

sydney faith

to all the wonderful people i've
encountered in my life.
i owe my words to you.

contents

prelude

sydney faith

seven point six :

from behind yellowed clocks in high-up
towers, time slows and rings in long,
unforgiving ticks. the city sleeps below and
everything remains untouched, like
freshly-made paper mache,

waiting for morning to come to send heavy
hearts to crumple what peace remains. sun
rises and heartbeats become synced to the
dangerously simple symphony of the
machine world. eyes ache to be renewed
and yet refuse to look up, forever focused
on cracks in pavement and laces on shoes.

seven point six billion strangers.
wanderers. patchwork personalities.
mouths asking to be fed. wearers of masks
and hearts on sleeves. searchers of saviors
and dull-day remedies, something to
awaken sleeping heartbeats that yield to a
routine guided by stoplights and to-do
lists. citizens of the in-between,

filling days with temporary sweetnesses to
postpone the heaviness of being human.

savior complex :

(a letter to those who want to save the whole world at once)

i know you worry too much.
i see the way you fight electric nerves
inside your limp and tired limbs.
i notice fingernail marks on red palms and
grabbing of frayed sleeves.
i feel the weight of tapping legs and quick
shaky breaths.

i admire your courage, but you must
remember that you cannot lose yourself
completely to the weight of the world,
because there will always be someone to
save and you will burn yourself out before
you can begin healing.

some days,
all you have are calloused palms,
tired eyes and a heart to match,
and the best you can do is soak up salty
tears from friends who are also tired.
you can hold their hand and breathe slowly
until tomorrow comes,
and although your superhero tendencies
are admirable, that will be enough.

your best does not mean your human
entirety.
keep yourself.

titanic :

when he played,
he left behind pieces of himself,
went many places
and only came back from some.

wore dark eyes that seemed to tell
his whole life he's been mostly lost,
with so much to say and no words to say it.

filled-in circles on lined pages mark the
peace of the artist -
wordless soliloquies that rarely reach the
audience, only heal the composer.

in dim rooms where lovers go to remember
or forget,
music fills the air and begs to be more than
background noise.
the crumpled man behind the keys asks to
lay down burdens,
yet still, dewy-eyed chatter crowds him,
and notes written to be listened to go
unheard.

they'll never understand its power until
only silence remains.

a choir of a thousand voices sunk beneath
blue waves, ripples of surface peace born to
few ocean watchers and believers in hollow
shells that carry the sea.

(notice the music while it plays)

atlas pins :

she wore running shoes with paradoxical
white soles. shoes to not only escape the
chaos but take hold of it, claim it, and use it
as fuel to keep moving forward. shoes to
take her up hills and across bridges where
she could exhale and set free the heavy
things she'd been given to hold.
she wants random in the most specific way.
she wants to fly through perfect clouds and
wear flowered skirts, visit blue cities with
unblue people. atlas pins mark the places
she wishes to run to and soak up. she
wants to be changed by her races and
peaceful at their destinations, victor of the
breath of relief that lies at every finish line.

always leaving,
a temporary citizen of countless worlds,
starting her own souvenir collection.

journal entry no. one :

i wonder if angels are ever unimpressed
from the other side of heaven.

when lovers part :

when tongues turn sour with tired words
and eyes look up to ones of a stranger
who has simply become conversation-less
company,
when point a and point b become too far
apart,
let these broken hands hold goodbyes,
force these tongues to remain heavy with
the weight of words unsaid.
make these legs unmoving,
don't let them run back.
let stolen music replace the sound of crying
wishes,
allow synced heartbeats to become faint
until you can no longer hear them ringing
in your ears.
scrub the residue from the city and sky
with every blink of stinging eyes.
remind yourself that the little things do
indeed exist and,
as much as you think you want to,
don't let yourself forget.

ghosts :

the little girl in her rosy easter dress,
the dancing child afraid of the dark,
the crying dreamer awakened by familiar
monsters,
the smiling wearer of ladybug rain-boots
and a yellow jacket,
the shaking youth afraid of never getting a
shot at normal,
the sweeper of broken teacups and patcher
of ripped kites,
the fearful mother awaiting an anxious
look in her child's eyes she knows so well,
the waltzing elder with wisdom cracking
her face,
the daunted stargazer searching through
invisible days,
the breather of today's air.

ever changing yet all the same.

rooms with more oxygen :

vision full of stars and heavy breaths,
here we go again.

i think this time i'll walk the art museum,
drive to the airplane park and watch the
planes grow smaller in a worryless sky,
or maybe buy some bubblegum.

i'll bring a journal to a dim coffee shop
and sit alone,
listen to music and cling to the lyrics.

i'll call my friends and we'll sit in my room,
they don't have to say anything,
we'll just watch breakfast at tiffany's in
pajamas.

my sister will bring me to a bookshop to
drink tea and my dad will hug me, and i'll
breathe a little easier.

i'll watch a video or read an article about
someone somewhere so very alive.
recklessly alive.

and oxygen will come easier to my lungs,
and everything will be alright.

miel to go :

i love the pre-day moment of peace that
asks nothing of you,

when cafes become meeting grounds for
perpetual strangers wanting to escape the
world that falls in white outside.

the small in-between minutes that bring
warmth to cold hands and shelter that
postpones the rush of the day
that lies ahead.
the walls that connect the crowd of drifters
if even for a minute.

i wish i could sit down for coffee with every
person in this world and ask them what
they love most, see the light in their eyes
they may have forgotten about,

but we're on our way to the greying
adventures of the adult world and we don't
have time to sit. inhale. exhale. absorb life.

we're just too busy.

emerald greed :

there may never be an excess of wonderful
that comes easy because we are all much
too human to be content with the
unmeasured joy that offers itself to us.

we will always want more.

the digital age :

we don't know the sour taste of envelopes
on weightless tongues,
or understand doorstep dates and
crackling vinyl.
fresh faces and freckles disappear beneath
unfit shades of cream.
love letters vanish with clicking timelines.
wandering children protected but lifeless,
sitting behind screens and begging for
genuine connection.
when emotional availability is an act of
rebellion,
we the professional dot-com dealers and
eternal wearers of rolled-down sleeves
watch life roll by.

we stand paralyzed as we watch the grand
reveal of the marvelous machine world,
built by our very own cold hands,
never settling for
r i g h t   n o w .

it's a shame these hands are so clean and
yet all these flowers remain unplanted.

when life won :

fragile wings protect steady minds
but wind and storm don't sleep to see birds
soar.
wide eyes become blurred by endless rain,
blinking poison drops.
bruises beg for a listening ear and find
themselves sinking more with every breath.

b r e a t h e .

you refuse to depend upon air, but without
it you can't fly.
so you wait,
with blurred vision,
for your dream of better days to drag your
broken bones into the sun and pour air
into empty lungs.
you wait for cold shining armor to open
locked doors.
you wait for dying flowers to hear the
weight of your words.
you wait.
i'm sorry we didn't see in time.

rest steady bluebird.

basil :

the potted plant that sits upon sunny
windowsill is wildly alive, growing bigger
and sprouting new leaves each day. how
ironic it is that its leaves will be plucked to
make soup to feed a man so devastatingly
dying. its life flows freely from its clay pot
while the man's life relies on drips from
clear packages into his arm. she makes hot
soup in the summer while her love waits,
lying perpetually in starchy white sheets.

he'll nod yes when she asks if he's feeling
better, and she'll learn to ache at the way
he lies to protect her.

someday, she'll stop watering the plant
but she'll keep the house on the corner
with the wasp's nest, where big love lived,
interrupted by a broken heart.

journal entry no. two :

it's a dream of mine that someday
some wanderer finds my book
shoved carelessly on the shelves
in the back
of a secondhand store
for twenty-five cents
and takes it home to read it
and feel seen
just like i have so many times.

old friends :

even though we're different now, we're still
very much the same. we like flowers and
full moons, and we're a little sad about
growing up. our eyes search for patches of
sunlight. our legs bounce with the energy
of anticipation, because we want life so
desperately, just different forms of it.

and if things continued the way they had
been going, we'd be driving on new roads,
me excited with the idea of new places
and you doing your best to hide that you'd
rather stay.

(i'll always be cheering from a distance)

letter to the lost at sea :

i'm sorry.
i know things are hard,
so hard and dizzying and all-consuming
that you're not sure how to function
anymore.

i know you're tired.
you feel weak, hopeless, anxious, and
stuck, battling between franticness and
despair.

i see the way you fight
and how much of your energy it takes.
i want you to know that every bit of it is
valid, and its periodic invisibility
does not change that.

but -

but how can i make you believe
in grape soda,
rain puddles,
jack-o-lanterns,
morning dew,
fields of daisies,
yellow-lit tunnels to drive through,
brick fireplaces in the winter,
good dreams,
and pretty futures.

how can i show you
the cinematic way
colors drip over the sky,
strangers in windows dance to favorite songs,
and dreamy steam pours from antique kettles
to make morning tea.

letter to the lost at sea cont.

we can go to the mall
like we did when we were young,
i'll bring quarters and we can get blue razz
bubblegum from the machines.
and there will be happy kids
playing by the fountain, making wishes.
we can make them too.

or we can drive,
drive so far away
until we reach the sun.
we can sit or lay or cry
or give in to the spinning world and dance.
we can just exist for now,
there's nothing wrong with that.

i'll yell from rooftops as many times as you
need that YOU MAKE SENSE!
and that i see you.
and that you are brave
even though you don't always have to be.

how can i convince you to stay
right here by my side?
we'll get you help and medicine
- not too much, just the right amount -
and someone to talk to,
and things will feel better.
it won't always be this way.

i know that i really don't know,
i could never know
how it must feel.

but i'm here,
but i want you here,
but i'm not going anywhere,
but you can talk to me as much or as little
as you need,
but i notice you,

but i love you.

please let that mean something.

white :

seventy eight degrees and snowing,
time trapped in slow motion bottles
beneath street-lamps.
white flakes turning to drops at the touch
of skin, landing on closed eyelids.
i can't save you but i will hold your hands
as snow falls and wrap your frozen
wounds.
you seemed to prefer bearing the cold
alone, as if you were ashamed of the way
you couldn't avoid it.

white air floating,
blue lips,
cold hands crossed to shield soft hearts.

jealousy of surrounding (noun) :

the pain of watching life unfold around you
when you yourself do not feel alive. when
the world breathes in green like april and
you're stuck in january. it's as if you're at
odds with the universe.

twelve :

she is confused as to why she can't look at
mirrors and make funny faces like she used
to.
she doesn't understand why her fingers
shake and grab at loose strings and
zippers.
or why the lights in her bedroom look
dimmer than they did last month, and they
don't get brighter when she changes the
bulbs.
why warm piano keys wait, quiet and
untouched, yet she can't bring herself to sit
on the creaky bench that lay before them.

she is sixteen now and reading journal
entries of twelve,
wishing she had understood her illness
better.
wishing she had fought the urge to avoid
glass window reflections and friday night
sleepovers with now only distant friends.
wishing the ink on old pages had not dried.
wishing she could go back and hold the
hand of twelve,
clammy and scared and wonderfully
(painfully) naive.

comfort zone :

you'll be brave and then go back into
yourself,
having glimpses of life that you've learned
to snap at, knowing joy only as a punishing
entity and fearing the impermanence of
butterflies.

you are happy on purpose and completely
scared of leaning into life. you smoke the
silence and beg for time to be kinder to you
than it knows how. you want heaven in a
box with a bow on top. you want to fall in
love intentionally and never accidentally.

but in doing this, your tongue has become
numb to the taste of snowflakes falling and
you don't cry at sad movies anymore.

you fall victim to this infinite lack of
freedom, a robot taking on the world with a
science to all things. the days are like
clockwork, wound back up every morning
as the sky floats into grey.

wake up. go to sleep. & do it all over again.

our mental addictions :

we are drunk on the virtues of today,
intoxicated by the feeling we are
accustomed to expect.
we are bathed in orange-bottled anxieties
that wrap our cold limbs, but we beg them
to warm us.
they are hungry and we are scared.
but we hold the very fears that hold us.
we will run from them if only on unlit
ground.
we are afraid of the sun because it leaves
nothing hidden.
we feel inhuman and broken,
stretched souls beneath grimy feet,
and our exhaustion grows.
we fall.
only to pick ourselves back up and try
again.
we are tired of trying.
it's as if we embrace the very cycle that eats
away at us,
hold onto the ugly truths because we don't
know what's outside anymore.
we fear the reaching angel instead of the
lying ghost.

we have become so used to bad days
and the glimpses of clear skies have
become so rare that we don't even
remember what they look like.
we lose track of time and space and focus,
but are too scared to dare imagine brighter
days, as if to jinx their possibility.
we fade.

(it doesn't have to be like this)

all the lives i cannot live :

if i could, i'd be a lawyer. i'd stand strong
on two feet in tight black dresses and speak
for those who need their stories told.

and i'd be a bookstore owner. i'd learn the
places where each book lives on the shelves
and i'd know just which one each
wandering customer needs.

i'd be a hot air balloon guide, blowing up
great big colorful balloons, leading
strangers through open skies, and listening
to their stories as they soar, witnessing the
crossing off of countless mental bucket
lists.

i'd be a taxi driver, businesswoman,
pediatrician, bakery chef, and seamstress,
in all the lives i don't have time to live.

it seems unfair how fast it all goes, and
how little we can do as it passes.
so for now, all i want to do is speak to loved
ones and strangers and write words that
are enough for those i meet. i want to
notice their wrinkles and scars and stories,
hidden like sun patches
in an old abandoned house
that nobody sees but everybody should.

i want to be a writer, photographer, diary keeper, art enthusiast. i want to be a professional conversationalist.

all i want to do is everything.

she will be free :

her friends paint her sky red, but grey
spreads over her world as if it could never
be washed away, a following fog.
she wears an ashtray heart, standing to put
out other people's pain and soothe their
wounds.
she does not believe herself worthy of her
talents and lends her canvases away.
she is applauded for her energy and never
allowed to be tired.
she is red but calls herself blue,
finding cracks in untouched mirrors.
she is a firefighter with a sleep mask and
no clean air, a master of closed-door
breaths of relief.
her hands are worn with blisters from not
letting go.
she is a painter, though she doesn't see it.
she paints stairs for people to climb up and
ropes to catch when they fall. she paints
stars in the sky when it's cloudy. she paints
smiles onto sad faces and flowers into dead
grass. she paints spring when it's winter,
sun when it's dark. she paints good into
bad and youth into that which is meant to
be young. she'll paint you a whole world
when yours seems like it's falling apart.

i can't wait for the day when she realizes
she can conquer the world.

she will be free
and let herself dream.

journal entry no. three :

sometimes, you travel
just to feel blue in new cities

and i think that's okay.

we can't expect new roads to always make
us more than we are at the moment.

from where i stand :

from where i stand, these borders are given
more power than our hands, which remain
in our pockets while others ask to be found,
seek to be reached out to.

from where i stand, our roots run deep in
contaminated soil, we sink blindly into
jealousy, comfort, and the principle of
difference.

from where i stand, it's much easier to stay
on the sidelines. it's much easier to tie a
blindfold around our eyes and ignore the
wars outside.

from where i stand, so many of us are not
willing to be weak, not willing to break.

but there are wars that require reckless
pursuit, and there are people who are far
too tired to continue fighting alone.

2007 toyota telescope :

sixteen and sick with the feeling that
windowless office jobs are inevitabilities of
the future,
finding peace from behind dirty car
windows,
and realizing that my heart beats slower in
january and faster in july,
when the sun apologizes for its months of
leave.

but for now i have the moon,
friends to drive with me under its light,
and time to realize that these big waves will
soon grow smaller and take up less of me.

for now, all that the world is asking of me
is to watch.
to notice subtle gifts,
the grey-lit space to breathe,
provided by a 25¢ moon to soothe restless
eyes.

interlude

sydney faith

journal entry no. four :

while we wait, life continues to move at a
pace unforgivable to those who seek to
catch their breath.

while we lie down, sun rises but hides
behind grey, and we miss the short window
where clouds turn pink.

while we watch, we forget to participate in
the small and secret romantics that days
carry silently, and no photographs are
added to dusting boxes. we miss red flags
and white lies and lighthouses that ask to
be seen.

but in the meantime, we smile and hold the
world for those who can't.

in the meantime, we draw on corners of
books and paint the walls blue. in the
meantime, we buy coffee alone and listen
to songs that feel like sun. in the
meantime, we stay inside to avoid the rain
but watch the street light up like day when
lightning cracks. in the meantime, we say
goodbye to friends setting sail on
adventures we wish were our own. in the
meantime, we decorate days with things
that will only ever be temporary.

in the meantime, clocks grow smaller and
we walk blindly through non-refundable
minutes.

& we ask them to slow down.

cage :

will you leave the city's cage
will you erase the old forgotten buildings
and watercolor skies
with their melancholy blues

if i ask you to fly
will you leave your chains behind
will you close your eyes and let your feet
drift away from the edge of yesterday

if i ask you to look for light to fill your eyes
will you open them wide enough to see
will you carry in yourself the belief of
things unknown

or will you box yourself in
will you lock your own open cage
will you guard your heavy shackles
and never step forward

100 days of clouds : an experiment

(the highlight reel)

months of getting better at looking up,
admiring.

next - destination anxiety (noun) :

the suspense that accompanies the in-
between. often found on elevators,
crosswalks, or airports, and in the sounds
of the clicking of pens and ticking of clocks.
the perpetual anticipation of what comes
next.

the part of the year when flowers grow
again :

transition from autopilot to aware, from
grey to color on a tuesday in march

postlude

madi hope

(written by my beautiful sister madi hope - whether she's behind a
camera, canvas, or piano, she's conquering the world)

as sky breaks :

as grey dawn lifts its rosy face, tired eyes
take their last look of the world.
air meets lungs as if for the first time,
dew latches to tired lashes of lost children
running from home to haven.
when light cracks through hidden blues,
minds buzz to action.
small hands ask to be held,
widowed hearts long for love,
and the world presents its vastness to
newly birthed eyes.
when sun streams though frozen windows,
bones creak to life,
feet carry music to the streets,
dimples rest in worn faces,
eyes give life to undiscovered colors,
and forward steps are taken towards
tomorrow.

october :

when silver hills come into sight, hourglass
sand drips slower
& life is found again in glass-bottled soda
and candy necklaces.

i will climb to the tops of buildings and
peaks of mountains even though fear exists
at these heights.
because what would life be if i stayed on
steady ground?

from way up here, there are clips of life
that you'd think only exist in the movies,
characterized by blue denim & red lights.
the city moves with choreography &
cartoon people set foot to conquer blurred
days and beat the sunset home, where love
lies waiting.
the view is great, but i'm just learning how
to climb and trying to wear a bigger brave
than i know how.

don't look down.

encore :

i am playing to a theater of stars tonight.
my friends have gone and all they left was a
torn postcard and a get-well-soon balloon.
there will be no encore, no great finale, just
a quiet bow and the sound of heels echoing
as i walk off the stage. i'll pack my bags and
say goodbye to the empty theater that held
my words until they were ready to move
on. painted glass casts shadows on the
silken stage where i begged to find myself
in each character. but tonight, i'm playing
to the stars. i'm playing to an audience of
one, stripped of every wrong answer i
begged to heal me. i stand before the world
without all the unnecessary add-ons of life,
and i've never felt more free.

journal entry no. five :

if we all wore masks, would we end up on the same bench?

(grievances of the modern time)

a letter :

(to all my heroes, writers of medicinal books and speeches, and fellow conversationalists)

there are few whose words seem to repair
the wounds of the world, sew them up and
stop their bleeding. words that know their
way to souls and are familiar with sinking
deep. i've always wanted to be one of those
people, but don't we all?

some days, though, my words are charged
with a discontent only leaking hearts could
create.
i'm sorry for the pain i've caused and the
hurt i've protected.

thank you for your words of
encouragement, of support, of love.
thank you for speaking truth into places of
fear and pain.

your words hold a power you may not fully
understand.

all the great nothings :

the view from the top of a peak is
spectacular, with nothing but water
stretching for miles.
there's the nothing that hides in quiet
bedrooms and airplane seats, the nothing
required of you, the nothing else to do but
breathe and collect thoughts.
the spring-like nothing after being chained
to some disastrous fool's gold, that smells
of sea salt and self-confidence and reminds
you what it feels like to understand the
phrase 'not a care in the world.'
then there's the nothing that lingers in low
places; the nothing left to do when all
options have been exhausted, the dead-end
nothing that follows countless days of
unanswered questions and unfelt life, the
nothing left to give away.

this is a harder nothing to face,
but while you have nothing left to give,
i have the world to spare.

heartbeat house :

there are veins in these walls, pulsing with
the energy of promise,
covered with robins egg paint and
memories held up by double - stick tape.

this roof is forever arched but parts of it
bend, yielding to the heavy drops of rain
that now fall to conduct an orchestra of
silver buckets.

the chimney blows cool air from blackened
lungs, heating children's frost-bitten
fingertips, small and blue and knowing
only how to grab at life.

unshaded windows look out to carefully
crafted snowmen.

sitting on the mailbox, delicately laced
twigs protect learning wings, and the
letters inside wait patiently to be opened.

these bricks are called Home, laid to create
a feeling of infinite love.

eighth st. north :

(& the places that built me)

someday, i'll come back to these spots.
i'll be seventeen again and wonder if my
dreams are too big. i'll take my new
favorite song to the street that offered
peace to a wanderer with little sense of
direction. i'll walk the block with a journal
in hand, taking note of the perfect brick
houses and top-floor apartment units with
gold banners and plants in the windows.

i'll fill my lungs with the reckless air of
youth and be reminded that these pockets
of peace will always exist if you're paying
attention,

and that these moving parts
will always be here to make a home.

54

there is rest here :

there is peace in this home to be found
after long days, when weary bodies beg to
be still.
there is freedom in these moments, quiet
and unexpecting and holding the
possibility of reprieve.
this place is offering rest for the price of
your baggage, laid honestly at the foot of
the stairs.
there is moonlight in these rusty kitchen
windows, pouring onto creaky floors where
feet dance away worries.

the door is unlocked. will you come in?

the thief of everything :

i wouldn't be where i am today without
someone else doing it first
(a fact i despise to recognize but admit as truth)
without second-hand jackets and
previously loved books,
song recommendations and outfit ideas
courtesy of strangers walking downtown,
and advice from those who've gone before.
i don't know who i'd be without these small
things.

all we do is emulate,
kidding ourselves that we do more, that we
are untouched by the outside world.

absolutely nothing is original.
write down lyrics and quotes on stolen
napkins, repeat interesting sentences
heard from strangers' lips, take dead love
notes and old postcards from empty
streets,
live through the eyes of someone who
knows their way to the sun.
don't be afraid to accumulate life as you go,
there is no copyright on these days.

journal entry no. six :

if you seek to be human, you seek to be
heartbroken. there is no perfection in
human nature or love.

(what are you willing to suffer for?)

space :

the distance between you and me.
the blue dome above our dizzy heads.
floating seconds dripping from our eternal
clock.
the half-inch between your parted lips,
waiting to say something.
say it.
this world is flooded with space, yet our
lungs shrink to make room rather than
sharing air with our neighbors.
we are self suffocating and slow to blame
ourselves.
bend the bubble you etched in the space
around you so that you may reach out and
hold another's hand.
stillness in space signals yet another fear
taking victory in yet another life.
space is a worldwide equilibrium, not a
keepsake.
let your guard down.

the romantic's best day ever :

it was the kind of day that you could feel
your heartbeat in your knees.

it was the color green of all shades ;
blinking lights of sunset ferris wheels,
skies filled with miles of seafoam clouds,
soft bright grass beneath wrapped hands,
twirling dresses and olive rain boots,
freshly plucked mint leaves for lemonade,
dark, calling forests,
floating music notes from crumpled pages,
hazel eyes staring back at yours,
melting blues lenses to green.

it was the kind of day that made you forget
every yesterday and believe in forever
springtime.

learning to pray :

teach me to wear these bones with peace
coursing through my veins. teach me to
sing when trapped words beg to be heard.
teach me to tear down borders of limited
love. guide my soul to another in need. give
me words and wisdom to heal the wounds i
encounter every day. teach my ears to
welcome convictions and respond 'yes &
amen.' teach me to not just hear but to
listen and let words sink into my skin.
teach me to trust, as promises of better
tomorrows were never fulfilled until i let
them in. rid me of a mind focused on
comparison and turn my eyes upwards.
teach me to open my hands to my
neighbors. give me reminders that the
world is beautiful if you take the time to
notice.

amen.

eternal butterflies :

the stomach flurries came and went until
one day they stayed and asked you for a
commitment to take care of them.

we are comfortable with the often expected
impermanence of life : there will be
another opportunity, these wounds will
heal, and tomorrow will come. we can
always walk out.

but the butterflies are asking you to feed
them. you have found in you the gift that
makes your heart quicken and ache to dive
deeper into this life. you've awoken your
creative spirit. will you let fear steal it from
you for the promise of comfortable
mediocrity?

my dear, i have decided upon eternal
butterflies. i have agreed upon forever joy
and i refuse to give that up. will you stay
and let butterflies remind you of the peace
of passion?

who we are :

we are pieces of each other.
we are lyrics from songs that held us when
the world was spinning too fast or ones
that carried our arms up when fast tires left
miles behind, floating in free air.
we are sunday morning coffee and
childhood music boxes.
we are imitations of players on a screen
and laughs of the ones we love.
we are the way we write our y's on paper
and the places we go when tomorrow
seems too far away.
we are each other's keepers.
we are the found keys to unfit locks and
catchers of floating away balloons.
we are reread postcards and collected key
chains from new destinations explored.
we are each other's heroes and
heartbreakers.
we are completely and beautifully
unoriginal and yet wildly unique.

and today, we are free.

life flutters (noun) :

the feeling that comes when you're exactly
aware of life.

can be caused by :

- sunshine
- sitting on roofs
- seeing other people happy or in love
- being proud of someone
- a really good waffle
- doing something you never thought
you could do
- finding songs and friends that seem to
imitate the sun
- puffy clouds
- fall colors
- bottles of strawberry soda
- reading notes in the margins of old
books
- getting letters in the mail
- the month of september
- et cetera

persephone of 20th century suburbia :

she's the queen of contradiction,
citizen of the in-between,
waltzing with daffodils in the underworld
and expecting the sun to shine.

she's a free-spirit chained,
the darkest shade of green,
self medicating with peach tea,
gummy bears, and her grandmother's
coziest sweater.
her oxygen is laced with lemon
and the whole planet wants to live in her
world.

but all i can think when i see her is
you superhero, you,
with your fraying floral cape & dark circles,

i hope you're doing okay.

jukebox yellow :

we, too, will soon see things so
indescribably wonderful. we will be alive
and find this life in every little thing;
hiding in teacups and train rides and new
lyrics that say what's been waiting in a
lump in our throats. our skin will buzz with
the anticipation of the next moment, but
our hearts will be calm, wanting only
exactly now. we'll run as if we're still
children and love bigger than the time
before, when we were too scared to. we'll
be recklessly intentional and utterly
foolish, for This, this moment right now,
will always be the time to be stupid and say
what's on our minds. sure, we can live
quietly and wait for adventures to find us,
or we can go, seeking every single thing. we
will expect nothing less than life. and when
it rains, we'll celebrate the fresh start it
brings.

no bad days.

here's to the young :

here's to magic christmas mornings too
excited to sleep, to dandelion bouquets
brought back to happy mothers, to seven
year old dreams of becoming a famous
actor and going to mars. here's to wiggly
teeth and being the queens & kings of
willow trees. here's to being foolishly
honest. here's to pink walkie talkies and
bike ride battle wounds. here's to dancing
on top of feet and learning to blow bubbles
with our gum. here's to unmasked eyes
learning how to carry the world. here's to
the young.

2020 hearts in windows :

sign of the times : busybody becomes a
term of the past and paper hearts become a
signal of life from the people on the other
side of glass windows, reminders that
wonderful things always find their way into
bad situations.

although scared, we're paying closer
attention. allowing space to breathe, time
to think, a required and needed step back.

and yet it's still the unromanticizable time :
when lives lost go without proper
celebration, when doctors grow extra tired,
and sick lungs fight for air.

we are moving still,

just slower,

and from a distance.

(oh, how i look forward to the day when i can hug my
friends and sit down for a cup of coffee. i hope to never
again take these things for granted)

fourteen // learning to read :

this apocalyptic teen angst,
fueled by salinger, rilke, wilde, fitzgerald,
and plath,
that's so utterly important for growing up
and realizing our worlds are only so big.

these old books,
with notes in their margins left by kids of a
different age
and being unconvincingly pretentious
while reading them
from behind pink booths of bagel shops or
alone in parks that are just becoming green
again.

these favorite stories
that showed me the language of those i love
and made me believe in worlds bigger than
my midwest bedroom.

these old words on frail pages
that helped the winter days pass
and taught me how to break
without trying to hold all the blue of
january within myself.

(thank you)

the man who walked :

every day, he packs up his things in a cart
and moves along,
never stopping long enough to make it a
home.
argentina to alaska and few visible signs of
exhaustion.
he came to my spanish class this winter,
and he looked simply alive.
i admired the look in his eyes and his
commitment to interact with the world
fearlessly.

i envy him and often find myself falling
victim to the idea that growing up means
giving these sorts of dreams up.

how cool is it to simply *live*?

i'll be forever searching for stories worth
telling, hoping that one day one of them
will be mine.

looking back on paradise :

abandoned places, lost in paper cities.

train cars where young kids once sat
excitedly in on their way to visit their
grandmothers
and where grandmothers once held hands
with grandfathers,
now empty with the silent weight of stories.

churches that once were filled with song,
now left with broken stained glass and
decades worth of vines growing down the
pews.

houses where young love grew old but
never shrinking, where fresh bread was
baked for children coming home from
school, where christmas trees sat blinking
with old colored lights, where babies grew
up to be brave enough to leave yet soft
enough to miss its comfort. childhood
homes, where young kids learned to ride
their bicycles and play guitar in their
rooms with floors now grown through by
flowers.

abandoned places, stories lost to the
artistry of nature.
grown out of, left for passersby to ignore
and wanderers to notice.

seventeen :

we the drifters,

wasting time in cars, driving around
windows-down to find blue raspberry
slushies, neglecting the freezing air as we
throw our hands out the sunroof and
scream.

leaving notes on receipts signed with
smiley faces,

dancing foolishly to spinning records and
thinking we are oh so cool,

waiting for trains at the tops of parking
ramps,

sitting by rivers building our futures,

spending midnights in pink neon diners
drinking strawberry milkshakes,

lying on rooftops watching the sunset and
thinking life is always more of itself from
these small heights.

romanticising days spent drinking grape
soda and rose lemonade and the one
summer we found them in a lake town
grocery store,

searching for new or abandoned places and
melodramatic songs to fill our loser
playlists.

professional stargazers, enthusiasts of lapis
lazuli nights spent in tents, backyards, or
on well-known roads.

rose colored and young with the impulsive
need to be absolutely alive.

dizzy and intoxicated by the lemon sheen
that we will always be this free.

untouchable, forever blue skied, with worn
denim and old sneakers for armor.

too young to know about forever but
willing to promise it.

collecting the world in photographs that
prove that for a moment, everything was
effortlessly wonderful.

grandma's apple pancakes :

3 eggs
1 cup of flour
1 cup of milk
dash of salt

stir together

pour batter onto warm pan, add apple
slices

flip

enjoy

the simplicity of sleepy-eyed saturday
mornings growing up

journal entry no. seven :

at the end of the day, there is still green
grass growing somewhere and somebody
just found their rose colored glasses.

that's enough.

writers :

we fight. we stare at blank pages for hours
and allow words to spin inside our heads
until they feel ready enough to flow onto
paper. our hands shake as we clutch the
blue-lined pages that hold the shadows of
our beings. we want to be freed by our pen
and the ink that runs from it. we guard the
home these dreams built, the words that
raised us, and the fresh air that fills our
searching lungs. we speak to stars and run
from the mere survival that binds so many
to the accepted inevitable, the one we can
read in their eyes when they tell us how
their day was. we chase the addicting
feeling of freedom that comes from
finished letters and empty cups of tea. we
beg today for its purest sense of life and we
stretch our palms up towards quiet,
cloudless skies.

and onto eternal tomorrows.

walden :

we want to believe in infinity, in beautiful
waters with no end and forever promised.
we want to dive & never hit the bottom.

but instead, we're just constantly leaving,
saying morning goodbyes to the ones we
love until we say our last. we're putting our
hearts on the line to faces of future
strangers.

we've perfected the collective brave face,
the silent commitment to ignore dead
ends. it's much less painful to be a reckless
optimist, intoxicated by the taste of
naivety, than a cynic, drinking poison
truth. it's easier to believe in small
eternities than endings.

so we hope
and live forever in a day.

journal entry no. eight :

bad decisions by the strokes plays on the
radio while my friends and i sit in silence,
asking nothing of the night, and letting go
of the frantic attempt to keep time from
losing itself.
fire trucks pass by with an urgency that we
don't have,
flashing red while we wait at the light.

we're slowing down.

we drive past kids in a loud blue
convertible
and realize that we aren't the only ones
who are so very alive.
it's the same feeling as when you're
watching the stars or you're walking
through new york city,
small but strangely comforted by the idea
that we are just a tiny speck
in a big swirling world,
and we are not as in control as we think we
are.

learning the language of iloveyou :

cups of coffee brewed by mothers
who later work for hours to get out the
stain its spill made on your favorite dress,
ice cream and bouquets of flowers
delivered by friends,
and blankets warmed in dryers by
grandpas
on cold winter days,
when you wish for a moment
that you could spend your whole life right
there,
the coziest you've ever been.

the convenience of distance (noun) :

the non-intimidating nature of space that
allows things to exist only as dreams.

to exist perpetually in the "distance
between" but never brave enough to end up
somewhere. living in limbo.

eliminates risk of painful reality but
sacrifices genuine human
connection / interaction.

attention to detail :

today, our reflections wait hanging on
walls and in our pockets wherever we go.
today, mirrors are impulse items, fluent in
the language of expectation.

but once, they were objects of discovery.
born on the surface of waters, molded into
obsidian rock in the mud houses of turkey,
shaped into hand-held tools that fit in our
pockets. the craft was rebellious, fueled by
curiosity.

i wonder if the first makers of mirrors
intended for them to be so powerful.

rewind & play it again :

dear dad,
stay this way, right here.
you'll throw me a football and laugh at my
athletic inability, and we'll soon go inside.
you'll make me a grilled cheese and while
you're washing the dishes, you'll tell me
stories of when you were my age
and remind me to feed my soul.

you'll play music and i'll dance on your feet
in the living room before going to bed.
in the morning, i'll open my windows with
sleepy eyes to wave goodbye as you drive to
work.

and someday, i'll be years older,
sitting terrified on an airplane.
the world will be spinning and i'll wish
you'd be there, holding my hand until
yours goes numb.

but i'll soon learn to swallow the lump that
comes from thinking about the way that,
even though you hope it doesn't,
time marches on,
and dads grow old.

but please stay right here, just for a little
longer.

ivory :

my little sister grace, whose name indicates
undeserved goodness, sits down every
afternoon to practice her piano songs.

she often dreads it, and only retreats to the
creaky bench after several efforts made by
my mother to nag her there.

she plays with nervous fingers that are
learning their way to the keys but knows so
little of the impact of their sound. she
creates music that travels to my mother's
happy ears as she cooks and finds me
doing homework in my room. it brings
smiles to the busy faces of my family. she's
is critical of her imperfect art, but doesn't
see the way it stands as a soundtrack to our
family, melting the worries of the day with
a clumsy, beautiful lavender's blue.

being an adult apparently means
weeks on end when everyone talks about
long days
& no time
& everything blurring together
& having to work in the morning.

it's the transition between
thinking too hard about
what makes you cool
to thinking too little about
what actually makes you feel alive,

and it's sort of exhausting.

but tonight.

tonight is thrifted mugs
of cheap peach wine
& violet cracks of lighting
& poetry that's not childish.

it's friends in borrowed sweaters
& spinning records singing
songs never heard
& wanting to remember life how it is
right exactly now.

it's one of those precious
small breaks in time
when the constant next thing disappears.

there's no unfinished work
or unanswered emails,

there's just people,
happily intoxicated
& recklessly free.

art amnesia (noun) :

produced by the overwhelming amount of art in the digital age. we often forget the things that once inspired us, and great, important things get lost in the sound.

symptoms include : creative numbness, lack of passion, or inability to see the artist in the art.

can be cured by a focused intention to shut out outside sound and absorb/interact with/take part in the art world or prioritize a daily dose of medicinal art.

(put on your shoes & head to the museum!
you don't have to do anything there, just exist -
see something bigger than yourself)

white flag waving :

thy will be done.

(taking a step back)

dead roses from back home :

today, i'm tired and sure that this city's not
my own, but tomorrow i'll notice the
dimpled smile of my ten year old sister and
promise myself to never leave. i'll regret
the distance, because even when we hope it
doesn't, time passes differently in these
two worlds. when i come back, she'll have a
new smile and a heart that is learning to
break for new things. i'll miss our after
school walks and our sleepover talks about
lives much bigger than our own. i'll miss
goodnight hugs and late night dance
parties.

the great unpackables : books, baby
blankets, piano recitals, and homemade
meals that don't fit in cardboard boxes.

but staying was never an option for beings
composed of such chaotic matter.

so i'll go, marching in white sneakers and
clutching a compass. though i love this
place and it will always be my home, i
cannot wait patiently for life to find me
here. i'll throw my cap with a crowd of
future strangers and hug my friends tight.
someday, i'll come back and go to my
favorite places, watch the planes fly in and
count the stars.

but there's still so much leaving left to do.

footprints :

you were born with every strip of time that
has come before.
you carry with you the pride of generations
past and to come.
you are the product of strong people who
made it through countless grey winters and
rainy seasons.
you are given a new sky every day so that
you may shape clouds and build staircases
into the blue.
you drip ink from the bottoms of your feet
onto maps,
atlases that mark the impact of those who
decided it was worth the fight.
you are incredible.
i am proud of you.
i hope you feel celebrated.

do well.

author's note :

if you've made it this far, thank you for reading. thank you for giving my young thoughts and observations a chance. the following pages are blank intentionally. i personally know the freedom that art provides, and i consider it one of the most important things a person can prioritize (even if you're "not really an art person!"). i encourage anyone reading to allow yourself to exist on the next few pages. it can be a journal, a place to make a list of dreams or gratitude, a chance to write poetry with no judgment, a spot to collect memories and doodles to look back on, a reason to pull out the watercolor set you've had for months & put it to use, a home for sheet music or your favorite caramel roll recipe, etc.

art is a beautiful thing, and we're lucky it's so easy to take part in its world.

i've always admired the way flowers
historically have been used as a sign of
gratitude for others' art, how they
oftentimes break the fourth wall in theater
and are given to those who made
something beautiful.

so, with that in mind,

flowers to you all.

(may your ribs ache from laughter and may
you always closely know the peace of art)

CPSIA information can be obtained
at www.ICGtesting.com
Printed in the USA
LVHW110035141120
671368LV00007B/379

9 781715 589899